So It Goes

Other Books by Eamon Grennan

What Light There Is & Other Poems
Twelve Poems
As If It Matters

So It Goes

POEMS BY

EAMON GRENNAN

GRAYWOLF PRESS

SAINT PAUL

Publication of this volume is made possible in part by a
grant provided by the Minnesota State Arts Board through
an appropriation by the Minnesota State Legislature, and by a grant
from the National Endowment for the Arts. Significant additional
support has been provided by the Andrew W. Mellon Foundation,
the Lila Wallace-Reader's Digest Fund, the McKnight Foundation,
and other generous contributions from foundations, corporations,
and individuals. Graywolf Press is a member agency of United Arts, Saint Paul.
To these organizations and individuals who make
our work possible, we offer heartfelt thanks.

Published by Graywolf Press
2402 University Avenue, Suite 203
Saint Paul, Minnesota 55114
All rights reserved.

Printed in the United States of America.

ISBN 1–55597–232–2

2 4 6 8 9 7 5 3
First Graywolf Printing, 1995

Library of Congress Catalog Card Number: 95–077950

Acknowledgments

To the editors of the following magazines, where earlier versions of many of these poems appeared:

American Poetry Review: "At the Falls," "From the Plane Window," "On Fire," "These Northern Fields at Dusk"; *Carolina Quarterly:* "Date" (as "30/4/93"); *The Cream City Review:* "Headlines," "Two for the Road," 1 [as "Smoke"]; *Field:* "Ants"; *The Gettysburg Review:* "Two for the Road," 2 [as "Shapes"]; *Irish Times:* "Shed," "Statue"; *The Nation:* "Bridge," "Cloud" [as "Not Standing Still"], "Passing Cold Spring Station," "Sons"; *New England Review:* "Angel Looking Away"; *New Myths/Mss:* "Through Glass"; *The New Republic:* "Border Incident," "What Doesn't Happen"; *Ontario Review:* "Outing"; *Shenandoah:* "Towards Dusk the Porcupine"; *The Southern Review:* "Firefly," "Visiting Mount Jerome," 1. *Alone* [as "Visit to Mount Jerome"]; *Southwest Review:* "Visiting Mount Jerome," 2. *With Youngest Daughter* [as "With Youngest Daughter at Parents' Grave"]; *The Threepenny Review:* "Glimpses" [as "Bits of My Father" 1 & 4], "Journey"; *Verse:* "Swan in Winter"; *The Yale Review:* "Stone Flight."

"Bat," "Birthday Walk with Father" [as "Birthday"], "Bubbles," "Couple," "Day's Work," "Ghosts," "Heirloom," "Night Figure," "Pause," "Spring Fever," "Wet Morning, Clareville Road," "Whistling in the Dark," and "Women Going," were first published by the *New Yorker.*

A version of this collection has been published by The Gallery Press, Ireland, 1995.

For the gifts of time and space, grateful thanks are due to the director and staff of the MacDowell Colony, to Bernard and Mary Loughlin of the Tyrone Guthrie Centre, to Annaghmakerrig, to the National Endowment of the Arts, and to Vassar College. Thanks, also, to Alice Quinn, Louis Asekoff, George O'Brien, Fred Marchant, and Peter Fallon. And, again, Rachel.

Contents

To the memory of
Evelyn Yourell Grennan
(1913–1990)
&
James Day
(1927–1990)

So It Goes

ONE

So we live here, forever taking leave.
RAINER MARIA RILKE, *The Eighth Elegy*

Statue

This boy is on the verge of walking
past me, about to go where I can't imagine
his whole body at one with itself
from the lips' full smile to the small
seed-bearing pouch between his thighs,
the muscled legs steady, ready to step
through any drawback or impediment—
even death itself, its wall of glass—
and not turn a curl amongst the bunched
unshockable waves of his hair: he is
a summary of boys, no one in particular,
the tight flesh at apogee, archaic
but recognizable (for all the remote beauty
of his nakedness, his vacant eyes)
as anyone's son on the cusp of manhood,
who will draw himself to his full height
and, holding both those wary hands
loose by his sides, consider in silence
the life that's brought him precisely to this
point of being born again, walking away.

House

Near the junction of two small roads
from where there's a wide, eye-dazzling
panorama of the bay and the islands that
shoulder out of it, I come across the site
where someone's sister's second cousin
has been putting up a place
for himself and his family, and I can tell
from this half-built rectangled shell
of bricks and mortar, from those
square vacancies where the windows
will be glassed in, and from the blind holes
made for the doors, just what a flimsy thing
a house is. Still, this one will be
soon finished, roofed and weatherproofed
against the storms that'll rattle at
its fast hinges, strain to separate stone
from stone, fling cracked roofslates
to the Atlantic, and roar and roar and roar
to dislodge into raw air
the family that would make its home
here, their lives hopefully opening
in this shelter, learning how to live
with one another and on this windy height—
a wired-in field of furze in front
and, at its back, the broad amazement
of the bay, the floating islands, the almost hourly
tilt and shift of stony light, or those
raving firelights when the sun goes under.

Passing Cold Spring Station

What you see is there's no second time:
the blown grass shaking like broken wings,
scarlet snapdragons in a plastic urn
unleashing a fury of flushed heads,
their child-lives supple and transient
as they face towards water
flowing fast as it can away. You sit

with your back to the engine, looking
at what's already passed—the pace
of its vanishing, how it stays to see you
disappear into the eye of distance,
wiped away like a tear
the wind brought on. Battered back gardens
whisper after you: *Remember*
rapture, the knotty pleasure
of its give and take, the speed of light of it,
how you were carried along. A sudden

congress of salamanders is burning
under a shower of spring rain: they lay
their fingerprints on stone, the faint
last spark of their pleasure
flickering into it, and out of nowhere
two swans appear
to be snatched back from you
by time and space, but revealed
still for an instant
as a brief presence among dilapidated reeds
and surely at home there

after you've been taken away,
your fugitive shadow only
the most fleeting stain on their air
who are possessed of all the light
that strikes water broadside

in a jumble of radiant exchanges,
no one lasting more than a moment's
breath or heartbeat, less
than the time it takes
you, going, to leave them go.

Outing

Granted the Atlantic between us, I can only imagine
walking in on you asleep in an armchair
the nurses have pillowed, your white-haired head
and the powdery skin of your face tilted sideways,
your chin sinking into the sag of your breast
where one button in the pale blue frock's undone.

When you fell down that Sunday last summer
and your poor shoulder buckled under you,
I could tell—trying to lift that terrible weight
from the lavatory's slippery stone floor—
the way things were. Still, as every other summer,
you loved our drives out of Bloomfield
to the sea, loved sitting in the car up Vico Road,
staring off over water towards Howth or Bray,
Greystones, the Sugarloaf (as plain on a good day,
you'd say, as your hand). And no matter
even if it rained, it was always a cleansing
breath of fresh air for you, a sort of tranquil
hovering above things, the known world
close enough to touch: blackberry bushes
and high-gabled houses; foxglove and bracken;
the hundred steep steps down to the sea.
I used to wonder if it ever crossed your mind
that the next life you firmly believed in
might be something like that—the same peace
of simply sitting, looking at whatever was there
and passing: older couples with their dogs,
salted children streeling from the sea,
a parish priest swinging his black umbrella,
the occasional brace of lovers in step. Over
the lowered window you'd smile
your genteel *Good afternoon!* to them all,
and seem for this little while at least

almost out of reach of your old age—its slumped
and buzzing vacancies, blank panic, garbled talk.

But now, near another summer, they tell me
your temperature flares, falls, flares again,
and nothing to be done. Alive, they say,
but in ways not there at all, you've left us
and gone on somewhere, and I remember
how as kids we trailed your solid figure
when you pushed the youngest in his pram
and turned to call us all to catch up, *Hold on
to the pram now, don't let go.* I remember
the pounding silence when you'd hide
and all of a sudden come dashing out
behind your voice—your arms like wings,
laughing our names to the air around us,
the sound of your glad breath bearing down.
But when I appear in a week or so, I'm told
you won't know me, the way you mostly
don't know the others, and I remember
your phrase when I'd come home at last
after months at school: *I wouldn't know you,*
you'd say, holding me away at arm's length
or in a hug, *I just wouldn't know you,*
only this time the same delighted words
will die in your mouth, and you'll be
two puzzled milk-pale hazel eyes
staring at this bearded stranger. You've left
already, knowing well what I've no words for:
the smudge and shaken blur of things, bodies
floating by like clouds, brittle sunshine
flapping through a window to your lap,
days in their nameless, muffled procession
or the frank night-scurry of dream after dream,
each with its seepage, bat-flash, dear faces.

Here, among the woods and hills of New Hampshire,
it's you I think of when I watch the mountains

appear and disappear in mist, the shape of things
changing by the minute. If you were with me now,
I'd show you these blowsy irises, and those
exploding globes of rhododendron, lady slippers
in the shade, or flagrant and short-lived the blaze
of the yellow daylilies. You could listen out
for the pure soul music the hermit thrush makes
alone in the echo chamber of the trees, his song
a blessing, you'd say, to your one good ear.
Side by side, we'd sit in this little screened gazebo
facing Mount Monadnock, and you might try
the mountain's name a few times on your tongue,
getting it wrong, wrong again, until
you'd give your helpless laugh, give up, and say
For God's sake don't annoy me, will you,
whatever you call it. Can't I just call it
Killiney, Sugarloaf, or Howth—what matter?
We'd agree on this, *God knows,* and you
would sit back to enjoy the view, the delicious
sense of yourself just sitting—the way
we've always done, we're used to—pleased
for the moment with what we've got,
and pleased at how that big green hill
swims in and out of view as the mist
lifts and settles, and lifts, and settles.

Night Figure

She hovers over the ache of thresholds: the brass doorknob
and the cream paint chipped at the jamb
enter her face again, so close she doesn't notice.

She needs to hear us breathing, three of us
pitching into sleep in the one room, tucked in
by a faint smell of face powder, sticky touch of lips.

Snare-beat of rain on the roof, the rain spitting
against the window. *It's spilling rain,*
she'll say to herself, *he'll be drowned out in it.*

As if underwater, she stands listening
to the house and all its stunned tongues
gather round her heart. Rumours of being

rush into the instant: a bus coughs by
on Clareville Road, quick steps
syncopate through rain, a bicycle bell

jings in the dark; *squeak squeak* of pedals
against wind and hill. Moving
into their front bedroom, she sees

from the window a hurrying figure, hears
the little brickish *click* that high heels make
on stone. A deep pain starts

to open her heart, and she's the secret
goings-on in hives—a slow gathering
and transformation, the finished, overflowing

golden comb. Nothing now, *nothing—*
till his key comes fumbling the hall door,
that sudden rush of air

as the door shuffles open, raw
against the hall's linoleum. Hint of stagger
in the hallway; heavy sit in the muffled chair;

his lidded eyes haze over, blinking: two hearts
are heaving like mad. Behind closed doors
the air listens to a huffle of voices. She can feel,

when the petals of pain and rage
have closed, her vacant relief: the house
complete at last; she can sleep. So

she lies beside his breath, her own eyes open
and the house a hive of silence
around her head, her splitting head. Fingernails of rain

tapping for help against the window: *Let us in,
let us in, can't you?* Then thickened silence
levels the dark, taking the bed

she lies on, and she slides—nothing stops her—
into the wooden dusk
of wardrobes, down the sheer drop of sleep.

Heirloom

Among some small objects
I've taken from my mother's house
is this heavy, hand-size, cut-glass saltcellar:
its facets find her at the dining-room table
reaching for the salt or passing it to my father
at the far end, his back to the window.

The table's a time bomb: father hidden
behind the newspaper, mother filling our plates
with food; how they couldn't meet
each other's eyes. When he'd leave early
for an armchair, *Just a glance at the evening paper,*
she'd sit until—all small talk exhausted—

we kids would clear the tea-things away,
stack dirty dishes by the scullery sink,
and store the saltcellar in the press
where it would absorb small tears of air
till the next time we'd need
its necessary, bitter addition. Now it figures

on our kitchen table in Poughkeepsie
and is carried to the dining room for meals—
its cheap cut glass outlasting flesh and blood
as heirlooms do. I take its salt
to the tip of my tongue, testing its savour,
and spill by chance

a tiny white hieroglyph of grains
which I pinch
in my mother's superstitious fingers
and quick-scatter over my left shoulder,
keeping at bay and safe
the darker shades.

Glimpses

1.

His morning-after in the bathroom,
the rank sweet-sour of whiskey-coloured piss
filling the toilet bowl I'd flush and hurry from,
holding my breath all the way downstairs
to the stunned breakfast table where he sits
in his unknowable aroma of self and soap,
aftershave, coffee, burnt toast,
chewing over the brackish crust
of some unspeakable remorse,
and glazing through the morning paper.
He'll cough, and the smoke
from his first Sweet Afton of the day
will lift, drift, and implicate itself
in the spills of sunlight setting fire to
the mute knives and spoons on the table.

2.

Once when I was small
and we were driving west
through fog and the long summer dusk,
he stopped on a hill
and we both got out
to go, as he'd say,
to the toilet in the bushes.

Land and sky had become all one
sea of blank in every direction,
and I felt afraid,
adrift, as if lost
and no home to go to,

but after a single wingbeat or two
had fluttered my stomach,

I knew
it was all right:
he knew the way
and would soon give me
name after name
for the places we'd pass
towards Carna, Carraroe, Rosmuc,
wherever. Comforted,

I climbed back
and felt the big seat tilt
as he sat his body in
and got the old green Morris
started, taking us on—
a tall father
younger than I am
getting us somewhere
safe for the night:

I was looking forward to bed,
morning in a sunlit strange room—
while he, maybe,
was tasting in his mind
that first pint and glass of Paddy,
imagining the banter
in galloping Irish, the way
he'd compose himself
at the strangers' table,
talk till the small hours
in a smokey kitchen. From where,

on the edge of sleep, I'll hear
his lovely helpless bursts of laughter
break out
of a throng of voices,
his own breath enter the world,
coming up to me.

Bubbles

We are—not forever but the moment—
blowing bubbles in the kitchen: the trick
is to catch these floating tears of light

on your tongue. My daughter screeches her joy
out the open door
as each one pops and leaves behind

the tiniest mite of light and soap, a sharp
quick shiver in the mouth. I'm reminded,
as we play this game of beauty and bitter taste,

how my mother, in the home of slow bodies,
would sing without smiling—every second Wednesday,
when the man with the accordion came—

the same song: eyes empty, a little glazed,
the microphone awkward between hand and mouth,
her worried voice almost inaudible

under the music. But bravely
she'd whisper-sing, her shoulders swaying,
until she got to *They'd fly so high* . . .

when the words would fly from her head again
and she'd hum the air, puzzled eyes
searching in vain while the others mumbled

a slow chorus, or stared off,
or just keep nodding, absently holding
any hand that's offered. She'd stop, then,

and sit to a sprinkle of applause,
the accordion crescendo, a whole galaxy
of burst bubbles ghosting the light

she shyly blinks at, those bright
brief nothings
marking, as they go dark, our little time.

for Anne & Tommy

Two for the Road

for James

1. *Smoke*

As if all the clocks in the house
had stopped: iron silence, thickening of ice,
the air abruptly grown stone deaf.

He's been disappeared, you see,
to a deeper silence, one world away
from the sound of Sophocles and Galli-Curci

or the racket in Mulligan's when he'd bend
headfirst over a smokey page
to read aloud by barlight, glasses off

and savouring every syllable. No sign of him now
in the mirror behind the top shelf
of winking bottles, nor even in the word

wound—"of unknown origin." He left behind him
on the kitchen table
a book called *Dusk,* one ink blue phial

of tiny pills, bent light in a bottle of Jameson,
a saucepan of cold potatoes with a spoon
against the rim, a pen and tightly written

notebook, open. Still life: the finished picture.

Wax-pale, his broad feet swollen, worn,
their sandals cast aside,
big hands laid open in his lap,
he sits cross-legged

on the dusty floor
between fridge and cluttered table:
dishes in the sink, dangle-bodies
of suits and jackets on a rail.

Weak light, tight shutters, everything
in perpetual shade: his fierce solidity
not yet beginning to disperse
across our lives like smoke

that twists and thins and vanishes
in tricks of light. In time
he'll be spirited away, leaving the house
cold as a cave, its mirrors staring into space,

facing down the long silence.

Behind a wall, someone is burning
last year's leaves, spreading their sweet

surrendered smoke all over. To breathe
the resined blue breath of it in

as dusk is falling, and in the air
there's no telling

the bats and the small birds apart:
creatures of the day and shade,

they keep dodging each other
under Jupiter—the only light

for the moment in the whole sky.

2. *Shapes*

You were reading of a people
whose syntax is the last
remaining structure in their lives.

You were writing, *Their lives
are ephemera,* when your heart
gave one long lurch,

looked back in a flash of pain
and stopped. But
the repose you wore

like a pilgrim blanket
said that nothing had happened in a hurry,
that you'd gathered yourself and gone

with all the gravity of a man
making a decision,
bowing with grace

to the weight of evidence.

From your commonplace book
the following: *There is
this quality in things
of the right way seeming
wrong at first. To test our faith. . .*

and I imagine
how you smack your lips
as you say it, save it,
shaping a little
saving structure

for our lives.

Wet December:
the stone room
and the roar of the oven;
the unoiled trolley
creaking under you.

Smoothly through steel doors
the white cardboard box
bulging with you: then,
up in smoke and out
on your own, alone

into the soaked Poughkeepsie air.

A gleam of Oxford rooftops
after heavy rain:

shapes take shape
in the sudden brightness

escaping from wet slate
and honey-coloured stone.

You always knew
the good lies we tell ourselves

to get by, their charitable
bleak syntax reaching

a friendly hand.

On Isis bank we scatter
the last of you
under a spreading yew:

green January
fitfully lightens the park
where a full-grown swan

stamps splayfoot
across the gravel path,
its wingspan fanned

wide as any emblem
over the sound of your voice
again insisting, *No symbols*

where none intended!

We rinsed our hands
in the river's icy water.
We wound our fingers

in the scheme of things
as it snatched you back
beyond our grasp

in a clouded solution
of stream and disappearing ash
from which we take

our hands back, burning.

Women Going

You know the ordinary ways they go
from you and from the stark daylight
staring through an open door. This girl
leans her lips to the beak of a dove
she holds against her heart as if
insinuating the best way out and back
and whispering, *Now I have to go.*

On a stone doorpost the young wife
arches her stopped body, one hand
flat across her belly, the other
raised to straighten the seamless veil
through which the full moons of her earrings
just appear, signalling a change of state
and no way back to the here and now
of things, to the honeysuckle open air
she's been breathing. The lady of the house

holds up one necklace after another
chosen from the jewel box a servant offers
and eyes the way it might belong
between the jut of her neckbone
and where her breasts begin, fitting her
for the road that opens ahead now
and night falling: *This one,* she says
at last, picking the pearls with a clasp
curved like a wishbone. And now

across the busy street you see a man
lean into the back of a taxi
where a woman's face is barely visible
looking back into his face and not flinching
as they dispossess each other into absence

and the door in that black cloud closes over
whatever they say above the roar
of rush-hour traffic. He bends away,

and you know when he looks again
she'll be gone, and in her place will be
this absence beating its stone wings
over every ordinary corner of the day
she's left, and left him in.

Journey

Get the word and go.

The river is waking:
the train breaks morning open over water.
Fleets of sleek sailboats bob at anchor.

Steely sheen. The green of the far shore
splashed with light. White
blouses of women
touching their fragrant patient bodies.

A tall bird bends
to its shiver-image
in water, refreshing itself
before flight. The river

runs down to salt, and the sun
of the summer solstice
transforms water
to one wide flash of glass.

Mortuary after mortuary
of spent cars, ghosts
of tenement windows
flapping plastic; the city
suddenly lapping my ankles
with soot and clamour

till the plane pushes up
through clouds, climbing
with streamlined heavy effort
towards the rarer medium:
we're leaving earth

and leaping into the clear
blue dome spread over. Below us,

a firmament of cloud
fashions a soft nest
for sunlight, bulky crests
of almost otherworldly weather,

nothing but radiance and shade
stretching as far
as the eye can see, a picture
of speechless peace, a world
that's not our world
yet we've come into it

as into some kingdom of tranquillity
where all our tears will be—
as they say—wiped away,
although this very minute
I might imagine

something still anchored
in her remains, as if
waiting for this face
to bend over her final face,
this firstborn voice to say

the word, any word, and let her go.

Whistling in the Dark

1.

The day of her waking and last exposure, I saw
the dark cloud of a tree against the light
and thought of the various ways a body had
of being invisible: all that solid wood and breathing leaf
washed out to an airy presence
in the dismembering energies of light. Later,
unprepared, I would see the breathless, full,
provisional rigidity of death, that loved body—lit
by its history—become a lump of wooden absence
wearing a flowered nightie and the ghost of a smile. Just
another way of being invisible: the temple stunned,
cheeks fleshy but cold as stone, locked hands,
and nothing to break the silence between us
but the sound of my escaping breath as it brushed
over the open secret of her *not-here, not-here.*

2.

At dusk near water I watch the waves, the luminous rain,
and a plover scurry over rocks and weed,
whistling to its hunger. Through gathering mist
the foghorn moans, and the rain hitting my head
turns me towards town again, which is all of a sudden
lit up, glittering, as if there were some pattern to it
after all. The bird prods a small rock, and I hear
the splash and wriggle of something alive under there,
a whistle of excited hunger. Silence. Then the blind cry
of warning off water. The world gets smaller and smaller. Time
to go home and I start, swallowing those big words as I go.

3.

When I stand with my right hand touching the back
of her crossed hands, I can tell without looking
that the livid veins and that bright traveller, the blood,
have settled for snow at last. Aflame once
in the friendly element of air, heartsfire beating in tongues,

they've fallen asleep in a snowbank, breathing a small hole
into the cold, and sliding in—as a snake in winter
makes a space to sleep and wake in. So, pulling the air
in their wake, these ardent pilgrims have turned
to a world of snow, leaving nothing but a little melt-mark
behind them, shape of a starched white nightdress
where tiny red flowers have all this while been blooming.

4.
Out early in the morning, I see ebony pellets of deer shit
glint with dew, and on moss filaments a few
first fractures of light. The white of a broken mushroom flashes
like a fish turning at the surface, or could be the gleam
of a piece of steamed plaice laid open before her eyes
delighting in it, the fork dipped, then wavering to her mouth,
all lost for one unfrightened instant
in the shriven intimacy of expectation, taste, the moister instincts
ticking over. From across the table, I have nothing to say,
trying to fix this minute among its poor relations.

What Doesn't Happen

Would you have raised your head and opened your eyes
and astonished us all with a few sentences of recognition
if I'd walked in anytime before the end and taken
your light hand in mine still hot from the journey?
And then died anyway, since there was only the one way?
I imagined something dramatic—me freeing you
from sleep, stopping time to get our stories settled,
but then I was looking up from the grave we'd laid you in
to see the tree in a heavy overcoat of green and everything
growing away like mad, a sudden blustering thundery rain
to remove all traces. So I speak in a low voice, knowing
I speak to nothing there, nothing coming through to here
where earth is covered in small translucent pods, the air
a congregation of feathered seeds taken by the breeze
to wherever they'll fall and, some, take root.

Yesterday I stood to look at a deer half-hidden in leaves,
a big doe still as a brown statue: ears cupped up
like dish antennae, her tail a white stain, the whole field
between us as I strained unable to see her eyes—only
the thick tan stalk of her neck, the head erect and pointed
in my direction, a scab of light in her brow's dead centre
as if something glowed there, the two of us facing across
that wide divide. Wondering would she scare if I went closer,
I started slowly towards her: still she stayed, not a flicker
of fright, just this tuned thing alert without trepidation
and watching me move through the grass in her direction
till I stopped, thought better of it, then edged back
to the path, my eyes still fixed on that steady glow
above where sharper eyes, I felt, were finding mine.

What's to be done with this desperate balance, this pendulum
to which even lovers are strapped in passion and doubt,
clocks ticking and seedpods clicking off our minutes? There is
no life I can put you back into, Ma—with your lipstick and rings,
your flans, fried cod and floury potatoes, your glass of Paddy

or Bristol Cream, ears eager for the same old stories, eyes
for the photos seen over and over; your rosary beads and your
seat in the sun, sweet tooth, love of summer—and I only remember
when we'd be together and I'd have to go,
you'd hear the finished day shut with a click, the door close
on you and on my voice saying, *See you tomorrow,* until that
last time, your hesitant surrendering wave through the window,
no more words. So now there can be no forgetting

your white hair and fallen breasts, the slack, soap-coloured
skin of your belly, slow feet on the stairs, or the way your teeth
grew darker, looser, falling out in dismay. But you would have me
keep in mind the good times, too—the times you'd say
I almost died laughing, or the two of us talking
in the warm kitchen, nothing but steamy diagonals of sunlight
standing between us, your ripe arms bare to the elbow
and the close air heavy with homely smells
of a chicken growing brown in its own juices, parsnips
mashed with butter and pepper, Sunday pudding. Now, here,
a sudden storm starts to clear the air, turning trees
heavy, impenetrable, with a novel green light, and I see
there's neither going back nor going forward, only this
running in place as usual, trying to see more deeply in.

From the Plane Window

Easy to see there's no living out there
on that seeming solid continent
of cloud, but in it I see two figures
running like horses in shallow water
and waving up at me, their dead weight
all shed, as if they ran
on the baked strand at Bettystown
that summer the sun never stopped shining—
my mother and my father splashing
by the sea's edge, white legs flashing,
the bright water breaking up at them
and fledging their ankles with foamy
platinum wings. All arms and smiles,
they're a ripple of skin and well-being,
waving for the invisible camera
and waving back to where the baby
sits in his pram on the sand
and squints out at their brilliant figures—
the way they break light, tossing
their voices over and over.

                 Now,
from the plane window I can glimpse
through cloud-breaks the scumbled water
under us, and soon we're in clear air,
all the cloud angels lighting out
for other regions: friendly and remote
as always, they'll gaze in our wake,
yawning a storm somewhere else
or propitious gales, but still keeping
a mild weather eye on those
young parents playing like children

by the calling shore, restored
to the pure possibility of their lives,
the long good day unfolding for them
slow as smoke in water, vivid
as a pinch of crushed sea salt,
and not a thing to be forgiven.

Ghosts

1.

One by one, in a fringe of frayed light,
they'll enter the narrow room
where you lie in the dark—a stone pressed
between chest and throat, a sting
of salt on the tongue—letting the fragments
reassemble. You'll learn to live
with the curtains drawn, the stammering
smallest breath of them remembered,
and everything you didn't understand
staring back at you
as pure fact, their closed faces.

2.

Sackcloth, the clouds come down as ash.
The scorched word, *Angel,*
drifts up the chimney. Nothing breathes
where the rose window
has lost its magic, dancers wither
into smoke, forlorn gums keep their teeth
agape in a glass of cold water.
And nothing in the dark
but a tuft of beige hair and a wisp of white
whispering at the window, *We have come
this far.* The air raw as a peeled turnip,
a vague turnip-coloured dawn
daubing the east, the shell of one bell
bringing the snifflers out
to eight o'clock Mass. At the front
window of the widowed house
a face—though you know it isn't there—stares.

3.

I can see the two of them moving
slowly over the sand away from me,
grown very small in the growing distance:

her pale blue cardigan; his olive green
tweed jacket; the slow roll of her hips;
his straight back. The light hovers, then,

till I see no sign before me, only know
they've entered into a last glimpse
of her hand reaching out for help
over a rocky place, and he stopping
at last and reaching his hand back
for her hand just as I'd hoped he would
before the sun went in and I have to hurry
from a coming shower. They have

become the barest glimmer, as if passed
through a glass wall in air, walking
on the other side of light. For minutes
I see nothing but rocks, the tide that
rises to cover them, taupe green and
navy blue tongues foaming closer. Then,

is that them again? Two tiny figures
float along the far wall of the pier
and are gone, nothing but a shaft of light
clinging a minute to the stone
until it too seems to shiver and enter itself
and go, a luminous late withering, leaving

me to stare at where it was. You take
what you can, even light on stone:
those two hands knowing their own
instant's touch, the exact exchange of that
before the loaded cloud comes over,
slows down light, and shakes it out as rain.

Through Glass

The figure I see stepping up from the lake
is blackened by light, erased
by the body of that big tree, and behaves
as a ghost might—flashing and black at intervals
till gone. Strange if my mother surged
on her own ghostly steps up from the water now
at a live pace growing closer, closer, until
I can clearly see the face she had, that bend
of the body, arms swinging on air as if,
renewed, they weighed nothing, the needy,
apprehensive, spreading smile
when she sees one window in this big house
is for the moment mine, and comes
confidently on, calling up to the glass.

Would it be any comfort to know the dead we love
are looking out from behind thick glass at us
who are small and quick as birds crossing the light?
They'd know our names, and the ways we had in their lives
of moving, sighing, pronouncing vowels, beating
two spoons together, opening a door. Or any comfort
to feel they stood in silence there, like people
crowding to the high windows of an airport terminal
—complete strangers almost touching one another—
to watch us going through the known motions:
simply taking in the way a wristbone winked
when light hit it, how a hank of hair fell over an eyebrow,
or hands were knotted behind? As in fact

my mother stood to look out the nursing-home window
the last time I saw her alive: standing still, still
leaning on the nurse's arm, she just *looked*,
as if by looking she could hold the moment
motionless against the flow, and then—like someone
surrendering—raised her arm and gave a little wave,
being but a speechless creature of desire as I am

wanting her to rise up the green bank from the lake
and find me behind my window looking down.

Already, however, the ghosts at the glass are turning away,
shifting their askance ache and shimmer of attention
back to themselves and whatever they're at
in their fluent state of indifference, a place—if that's the word—
where these words must stop and vainly circle. . . .

Visiting Mount Jerome

1. *Alone*

After I'd touched down last summer on my parents' grave,
clutching yellow chrysanthemums and small carnations,
I wanted to walk away on my own at last, without
their gone bodies grappled to my tongue, wanted them—
when I stepped back from their names and dates—to stay
where they were together and, as the stone says, *At rest.*
I was waiting for a sign, a ghostly touch on the shoulder

or a voice saying my name, something abrupt and decisive
to take my bearings from, a sense of something—freely and
from out there—*offered.* Of course there was nothing in the air
except that silence that's the regional dialect of the dead, their
mother tongue, its one functioning tense an inexhaustible
infinitive we can't unscramble, and I knew I'd come
to a border as distinct as it's invisible, like the line that crosses

ordinary fields without a mark but is impossible to safely
step over, where we were to let go, take leave of each other,
or at least where they'd let me away alone and I would leave them
be as they'd become—their own completed selves at whose
unruly grave I'm staring, and staring with that puzzled look
of expectation and repose my own child had when I held her
for the first time and she looked into mystery and

it was only me. All I could do, then, was turn from their stone
and move off among the other graves, remembering how, as a boy,
I'd be taken from them, waving, at the railway station, and how
I'd settle into myself for the time alone at school, something
winged with fright and exhilaration descending to nest in me
then, as it does now among the graves, when suddenly
and with not the slightest hesitation or strangeness I find

myself walking away, just like that, from my dead parents.

2. *With Youngest Daughter*

No candles, paper boats, nor any of the white acts of mourning,
only—diaphanous as a daylight moon—the dandelion clocks
blowing time away over the double grave we've laid them in.

The place in disarray: one lumpy rectangle of dried earth
the width of a coffin. Hawthorn and chestnut in blossom,
Sunday figures afloat among tombstones, ablaze

with carnations, irises, chrysanthemums. I read their names,
the phrases chipped in stone, and she says she can
hear their silence, then straightens our two red roses

in a stoup of water. When we leave through the strait gate
of what was once an apple orchard, she takes my hand and says,
If it starts to get dark or the path ends, will we turn back?

and before I can begin to imagine what she means
a lark hurls itself into a spell of grace and improvisation
over our heads, rising for an age of pure song that keeps us

speechless, looking up, until it flutter-plunges into silence
and clumped grass, entering the aftermath as we two enter
the outside world, her warm small hand fiercely holding.

Birthday Walk with Father

Eighty-one you'd have been. Given the fine day,
I dawdle the afternoon away in the woods
with binoculars. Sudden shapes of small birds
appear disappearing between leaves, delicately
peck at beech moss, nibble tree ferns. As a boy

you collected eggs from hedges along the Boyne:
only one a nest: prick it, blow the insides out,
save the whole hollow orb as trophy, laying
its speckles or solid colour in a hinged box
on cotton wool. Today, I see, the beech leaves

have begun to uncurl their little fists, turning
that pale translucent green you once described
as stained glass. Did they shine out at you
from early on, I wonder, speaking that gracious image
to your eyes? Stopping to look, I imagine

you stopping to look and thinking, *Just
like stained glass*—maybe a window you'd seen
in a chapel somewhere as a child, or at the seminary
before you gave it up, turned teacher, married.
So much closed off—not even a mystery,

just a blank map. Still, those gathered eggs and
beech-leaf lozenges of stained glass took root,
letting the two of us walk out together—almost
companionable along the cusp of spring—to meet
your eighty-second year, my eyes peeled

for the birds I spy on from a safe distance, hoping
I'll know their names and would be able to tell you
their true colours, the shape of their song, while you
keep your worried gaze on the ground—in silence
minding every concentrated, precious step.

TWO

And the world returns once more.
RAINER MARIA RILKE, *The Eighth Elegy*

Couple

1.
He is hearing out the crickets.
She leans back in a chair

so the light, creaking,
can find her eyes. She stays like that,

braced and at rest, eyes closed,
eyelids warm. On the porch of salt

he stands in shadow, feeling
the season fly down his throat.

His heart will burst. All he can say
is the leaves are turning.

2.
They'll have dinner together.
The little tongue of flame

will sing in the wineglass, the butter
be a glitter of liquid gold

running away
through pale green

asparagus fingers. The fleshed
wedge of swordfish

swimming in cream; a tiny
white dome of rice

on flowered plates. It will all
be there for a moment:

their murmuring talk, the child
asleep upstairs, their dim

reflections in the dark
uncurtained window, glinting

and leaning into each other
with forks suspended. The image

of lips moving in silence,
and that one tongue of fire

pulsing like a live thing.
The full particular

livid taste in their heart.

Pause

The weird containing stillness of the neighbourhood
just before the school bus brings the neighbourhood kids
home in the middle of the cold afternoon: a moment
of pure waiting, anticipation, before the outbreak of anything,
when everything seems just, seems *justified*, just hanging
in the wings, about to happen, and in your mind you see
the flashing lights flare amber to scarlet, and your daughter
in her blue jacket and white-fringed sapphire hat
step gingerly down and out into our world again
and hurry through silence and snow-grass
as the bus door sighs shut
and her own front door flies open and she finds you
behind it, father-in-waiting, the stillness in bits
and the common world restored as you bend
to touch her, take her hat and coat from the floor
where she's dropped them, hear the live voice of her
filling every crack. In the pause
before all this happens, you know something
about the shape of the life you've chosen to live
between the silence of almost infinite possibility and that
explosion of things as they are—those vast unanswerable
intrusions of love and disaster, or just the casual scatter
of your child's winter clothes on the hall floor.

Towards Dusk the Porcupine

Startled to see me
where he shuffles out
onto the dirt road between stands of trees,

he leans first into the ferns
and clumps of poison ivy
but then comes on, crossing, and I wait

while he levers his slow spiked amble
to the woods
on the other side

and into the depths
of his domain of moss and bark,
known shadows, rocks

bright-scabbed with lichen. It's
nearly dusk, but I can see
his body's chalky beige,

its black and white quills
pulsing, his blunt
pig's head tucked low,

and the targe of his arse
black as charcoal. On oddly
meditative steps, wavering a little,

he seems aware of bearing
the weight of his body with him
as he enters a crackle of twigs

and dead leaves, doing this undulant
slow waddle—fat Caliban—
into silence and the brown

living kingdom of shade,
his nodding small head
peering shortsighted

at the ground he's covering
hunched over—like Lowell reading.
Suddenly, he stops

to stare glumly back at me,
one brilliant quill of curiosity
taking in

this small walking tree at which
he nods once a bobbing head and then
goes deeper in, to be lost

among last shadows, forgetting me
already, his faint chalky outline
ghosting behind a white birch

into invisibility—knowing exactly
what he is and where, and how
he ends at pointed edges like that

and can cast them off
when needs be, his heart
in its reed basket

a full thumping, the twenty
species of beetle and seed
sweetening his belly.

Cloud

There comes in middle life a moment
when everything is very solid
and seems to stand foursquare
in its own hard, uncompromising light.
But soon it's the shimmer of things
that begins to grow on you, the solid
starts to waver, fold, dissolve, flow;
hills are just undulant lines of colour,
mobile as massy clouds that trawl
their shadows across a sea of grass,
and you can see the way the big light
races after shadow, and how things
live in both: metal benches, leaves,
a sky blue trike, the spotted
brass knocker on that green hall door,
a glint of rainlit kitchen windows.
And this is the moment
you start to catch the sound it makes
as it happens: passing traffic
and the stew of birdsong,
telephones ringing in different keys,
a door banging, all the babies on the block
in chorus, and over everything
the pitiless squeak of clotheslines
or a wind racketing in the fuchsia
or honey locust. When day darkened
we used to say, *The sun's gone in.*
Now we know it is the clouds
in their ceaseless, indifferent, high
bright life and shade, going over.

At the Falls

Although the lilacs after all that rain have all
gone rusty, the sun's brought summer back
to warm your hair, and brings these three boys
down to the river where the cotton mill once
turned its big wheel, brings them to the flat
rocks at the falls where the swollen water—
colour of tin and tree bark—dawdles slowly
first in its approach and then plunges over,
its darkness transforming in an instant into
light and air as it twists like bolts of cotton
till it strikes the line of jutting rocks and
fountains down and out in a bristle-arc
of wet light, a flare of flashy water unwinding
to the bottom, where it goes on recollecting
the vertigo of its last moment aloft, the odd
exaltation of its fall as it leaped, wondering
would it ever be the same, the same again,
and breaking then into a hundred hands
of light, before feeling itself start to be itself
once more—slowed down, flowing away,
changed and not changed but held again
between sensible banks, and not a thing
of wings and terror until the next descent
narrows its throat and it takes the same rush
through its whole headlong body, ready
to cast itself away again, surrender
to whatever in its own nature keeps it moving
between such formless / formed
expressions of itself, until it loses all
its vast accumulated life to salt.
                          In khaki shorts,
the three boys gleam like sea beasts, making
their ungainly earthbound way over rocks
to step behind the water screen and stand there
in that ear-numbing roar and reach their arms
out through it, stiff limbs hovering as if

disembodied, at odds with the steady state
of water-chaos that stretches back to when
first water began to make its creepy way
in the world, and map the whole outlandish route
to its own undoing. The boys just stand there
in the deafening bliss of water—bodies behind,
arms in front, an image of its bottom line:
how it will not stay, how we are behind
and ahead of it at once—their young triumphant
flesh in water, who have not surrendered but
know its near danger, *drunkenness of speed*,
the way it offers its endless assent to gravity
by going over, going down, some of it flying off
as mist, pure spirit in the shock of boiling
almost against its nature, while the rest becomes
a heavy froth of light unfolding, struck thunder.
                                                    And still
the eye's tugged back from what has happened
to what's about to happen, back to black water
with the luminous stain of tree bark through it
as it dawdles to the falls (*again!*) and then (*again!*)
taking the plunge, the rocks breaking it to brilliant
atoms of itself, another life if only for an instant.
Forgetful of their own flesh and pride of the flesh,
the boys stand still inside the noisy heart of water
and stretch their arms out, aiming crazy laughter
at each other, water striking and splashing
off their arms as if off fountain creatures
you'd stumble on around a cobbled corner
in Rome, and pause at the sight of the sleek
limbs of horses, thighs of gods, those glistening
torsos, nipples, fingers. Above the clamour
the boys are calling one another, convinced
they've entered and are at home for the moment
in the secret depths of this other element: still
the water won't stop and you watch it
refuse nothing, plunge and recover itself
from fall to fall, in terrible kinetic love

with gravity and going on, to rise somewhere
in fragrant dusk among jasmine and oleanders,
adrift, infinitely receptive and never-ending
like *the calamity of death*. It makes a music
you couldn't have intended or imagined, the ceaseless
stream of it brimming without intervals the air,
overflowing the ear, pure vigor taking its separate
self-absorbed life away in—always—the other direction.
                                        Now the sun
falls on the water and the arms projected
from the water, which will soon grow tired
of their own daring, this making strange of themselves
and the common element, and the sun falls
on your own head where you stand on the footpath,
warming your hair. As one who sleepwalks,
you sweat uphill again, find your way home
and fall into a deep sleep, your head become
one stanchless wound of sound and movement
streaming away, an opening to what could be
nothing but change, yet stands, a constant thing,
and flesh in the midst of it our signature, saying
we belong, saying nothing stays.

Day's Work

1.

Bent over in the stone garden,
the child tends forget-me-nots and fresh words:
Awfully, she'll say, and *Concentrate*,
turning her world around.
High up on the grey slate roof
a man fixes wire-mesh muzzles
over chimney pots of yellow clay,
while another—trousers tucked
into muddy Wellingtons—leans
a fork inside the sod, and lifts
this small mass of darkness: distinct,
the single clink of tine on stone.

A sudden hysterical bellowing of cattle:
flesh-coloured heavy udders
dangle like churchbells. Olive green,
the jeep circles the estate,
and on the lake's still surface
an emergency of inky insect scribbling;
copulation is a second's spin, a spasm.

Now the word *Soul*
seems more and more remote,
although day may tremble
on your freckled neckbone
with the weight of something
that won't add up—the way the scent
of laurel flowers flooding the avenue at dusk
rushes an episode from childhood on you,
that may not be explained. And still

people go on hanging out laundry,
laying garden paths down, as if these
most natural things in the world
had a world to come home to:

they've draped their banners
across the grass; in one thick even line
they've sliced the sod; sun falls, then shadow,
on the stack of paving-slabs out back,
waiting, it seems, for something to happen.

2.

This morning the methodical fog
was chewing things over: one by one
they disappeared: barbed-wire fences
pearled by rain; arched hay barns; the milky grass.
The rhododendron's naked blaze.
First to go was the ghostly
half-moon, a quick mouthful.

Remember the sea fog's rapid throat,
how it swallowed islands, cutting your own house
out of the picture? How it left
only the lowing moan the foghorn makes
a mile from the mouth of the harbour?
How you huddled in small low-ceilinged rooms
where cold faces are pushed
against the window: speaking in whispers,
comforting the child, almost afraid
to look at one another?

Bridge

High up in the clear between the paling half-moon and the lake,
the white belly of the ratcheting hatchet-voiced kingfisher
is a stroke of light as it pauses all of a sudden and swoops down,
then levels off, threading the eye of the small bridge
like a stunt pilot, and skimming with headlong grace the strip
of running water—loony topknot fangled, a flame, a fright—
and vanishing before its laugh does. A still figure stands
on the bridge, looking after: behind him three Canada geese sit
squat on their own cold image in water; some trees so bare
he can't tell whether they're dead or starting their winter sleep
that brings them round to raucous households again
and the crash of light. But a few roses face down the first frost
and are as wounds, or doors to what's possible in the fallen garden.

Last night, under cover of the dark, he could hear the throaty geese
carry over the house their saxophone grace and desperation,
and here this morning he can find no name
to allay the perturbation shaking his feet on the ground:
it's always the back of her he catches, imagining the clean
groove of her spine, the daily grind of bone on bone, not
a going away, but the stillness of a painted lady letting herself
be seen averted like this, for as long as he can bear looking.

Dusk yesterday—the day the highest tides in years had swollen
the river up as far as here and farther—he watched the water
curdle across the growing dark, saw it spate in great muddy rolls
and rush upstream, as if against nature. But what was he doing,
promising to walk the water north as far as it would take him,
to a place he could step over and never wet his foot? Here now
he sees light settle for frozen roses, and a kingfisher commit
acts of grace out of its loud hunger. Sees the half-moon give up its ghost
to common day. Sees a whole garden stiffen round a sundial
in shadow, the white snags of his breath catching at branches.

Bat

With no warning, and only the slightest *whishing* sound,
it was in the room with me, trapped and flying
wall-to-wall, a wild heart out of its element: flat black
leather wings that never stop, body become
a baby fist, tiny head blindly peering. Between its teeth

it needles a piercing, inaudible pulse-scream
that sets its course and keeps it beating, barely grazing
walls, wardrobe, chest of drawers, all—pitch pine,
walnut, Irish oak—smelling of outdoors, I suppose,
and sending it round the bend while I
try to follow its dodgy swerves, duck when it flutters at me,
fumble after with my eyes. This all happens

in a fathomless daylight silence which binds us
for a hypnotised little while, making me feel—
while the creature circles and circles—as if I'd been kissed
repeatedly in sleep, light lips brushing, gone. At last,

by luck as much as navigation, it flits through the window
I've scrambled open, leaving me
to track its zigzags over bright grass—by light afflicted,
desperate for the dark. Now, months later, I still remember

the way it went about its woeful task (trying to find
friendly shade, make jinking missions in the homely dark,
its heartbeat holding it to scents and glimmers
of bloodsap, wingwhisper, nightsqueaks, void), the sheer—
to my ears—stoic *silence* of the whole operation
saying how you behave in a tight corner: *Keep quiet;*
keep moving; try everything more than once; steer
by glancing touches, aftershocks, and the fleeting grace
of dark advances, quick retreats, till you find in your way,
with no warning, the window, open.

Headlines

I knock on the tree. It opens
into my mother's grave: a beech tree
coming into leaf. Wan green
springlight: one wind-up wren
clicking for cover, making her bed
in a tenement of dead wood.

The border crawls
along these little hills the ice
let fall; it could almost be invisible
but for just what happens:
one more bedroom mirror in bits
and shivers, the spreading chill.

'Victims,' they say, and 'killers'—
running out of words. The ice
waits for a change of heart. Here
is a girl's head, a man's hand
holding the gun against it: she feels
the small round point of it for a second.

Ordinary days. Spring's slow
explosions all over the place:
beech leaves, maybush, lacy
sprays of laurel, cherry blossom's
pink boudoir. Such a crush
of shameless life, you'd forget everything

except this jeepful of soldiers
patrolling the estate, buttoned-up
and clutching sten-guns. In her last years
my mother never read
beyond the headlines: *It isn't real,*
she'd say, folding the paper and going

back to her window, *how could it be?*

Sons

My son, fifteen, is playing soccer:
his lovely kneecaps ache, his breath
comes in spurts. He is flat out,
sweat slicking his face with salt.
The sun looks down on his body
and laughs. He will stand
steaming in the shower
for an age of bliss, becoming
water, remembering the quick touch
of flesh on the run, shuddering bone,
the sudden tumble-fall on grass.
But on the cover of *Time*
a boy soldier is staring out
from behind the thick muzzle of the gun
kissing his cheek. In the cafés
the mutilated fathers or ghosts of fathers
feel the round white tables shake,
small glasses chatter like bells: their boys
are killing one another under the stars,
kissing the stock, the long stiff coolness
of the barrel, the trigger's tongue, the little
black hole of a mouth. Mouths
of smoke, their dark hair
flaps like blackbirds, their beautiful
smooth bellies, falling,
for a moment, and a moment, shine.
Will they float home as mist
to the fathers crying off rooftops
or fly against their lives? I see the fear
that stutters in their breasts,
those little shiver-puddles of light

their eyes. They'll hear the mothers
call them from play, find their sleep
full of crooning and the small blue flowers
their sisters sew onto laundered sheets.
They can smell the fresh sheets—
their apples and saffron, their aloes,
their cinnamon, coriander, stone mint.

Horses

1.

Although they seldom muscled above me,
I remember being dwarfed
in the stone fountain of their force,
rawly afraid, awe-struck at something
vast, a violence harnessed and hauling
a cart of scrap metal through our tidy suburb,
men with wild weatherbeaten faces
snapping the reins. The neck's
thick branching grace I remember,
and the fleshed bones in their legs
that I saw from the footpath or, once,
watching a blacksmith bend to them
in a forge in Terenure, and lift one,
and fold it neatly over in his aproned lap
and touch the crescent foot
with a big file or pliers: the instrument
a glimmer in his blunt hand, the whole
horse-bulk rippling into shadow.
A few times, too, I felt tender rough lips
touch my hand that held, flat-handed,
a snatch of grass, fearing the teeth
but staying still until—grass gone
in a quick crunch—I had my hand back
to pat the silky nose, finger-comb
the mane, slap sleek hindquarters
and the belly big as a currach, to feel
the heat simmering there, the nervous
flickering along skin as if the veins
were charged, the blood itself electric,
and knowing how heavy the flesh was
from the way my hand lay on it
like nothing, a straw on water. I'd imagine
it all falling on me, or being lost
under a flail of hooves, the feel
of so much live involuntary flesh
capsized over my own bones

in a fury of bared gums, a trampling
froth-storm white at the mouth,
two black moon-mad eyes on fire.

2.

Remote, perfect, overwhelming
how they inhabit space
by crowding out the air they occupy;
and yet contained, confined inside
some glorious force field of their own:
a solidified smell of oats, sweat, leather,
contemplation, astonishment. The span
and ponder of them absolute
in anchorage, taut as propellors, steady
in that massive confidence of rump
and hindquarters, thews bulging, everything
sinewy, roped, rounded as seashells,
the grand parallelogram of the head
giving millstone definition
to the word *Skull.*

3.

Two white horses in a field up the road:
a mare and her colt gleaming
out of the clouded day, at grass
in a windless wide silence,
the tenderness between them palpable
as that mild and serious something
in an empty chapel. The young one
is lying down, while his mother
browses a close circle round him,
but when she stops to stare at
the sound my footsteps make
on the road beyond the hedge
at the edge of her world,
the little one rises too and stands
looking, his two coal black eyes

lingering on my strange shape, letting
out of his lustrous ebony muzzle
a faint, plaintive, interrogative
whickering.
               I know they're abroad
in every weather—wind snapping
at all corners of the valley, rain-squalls
making ditches roar, sunshine
cooking the air in clover—and it is for them
only weather, to be taken
with the same dense patience
they proffer to whatever happens, although
at intervals under a heavy shower,
after they've been standing as still
as creatures carved in quartz,
the mare will suddenly toss and gallop
round the fuchsia-bush and barbed-wire
border of their field, her colt
quickly following, his new legs
slow and a little stiff at first, but then,
with a springy, kicking bound
and a careless, elegant animation
of everything that makes the body
and the body move, he'll cut
to a perfect dash, tuck tight
to a tandem gallop, doubling his mother
on the run—picking up as he goes
whatever he knows from her,
but first how to warm the blood
she's given him, and then
how to be, increasingly, in the world.

Angel Looking Away

Somewhere
they are throwing rice and rose water,
carrying the coffins shoulder-high,

but on Pisano's pulpit the angel
is turned away in sorrow
from the slaughter of the innocents

and in the interrogation centre
a man has turned
away from the polished steel table

on which a man—
calloused tallow soles
stretched towards us—is twitching

as a live wire
wide as its own glitter
kisses the eye of his penis

while another man
is gazing down, perplexed,
at the naked figure on the table

and holding a small black box
with two switches: between
a thumb and tapered index finger

one switch is being gently eased
to the ON position, and now
the poem is looking

at the angel looking away,
at that handsome strong youth
in his marble sorrow,

and you know
it can do nothing
not to lose its tongue.

Stone Flight

A piece of broken stone, granular granite, a constellation
of mica through its grey sky, one chalky pink band
splitting slabs of grey, it fits snug enough in the palm
of your hand. Toss it up and it falls, an arc saying *yes*
to gravity again, and saying in its one dunt of a word
when it falls with a thump on the soft path, *I'm here
to stay.* At a pinch, you might strip things down to this:
compact and heavy the pressure on your hand; the light arc
as if things weighed nothing, casting off; the apogee
and turn, catching a different kind of light; the steady,
at the speed of gravity, descent; and then that dull but
satisfying *thunk* to stop, its cluster of consonantal solids
allowing no air in, no qualifying second thought
as it lands like the one kiss to his scratchy cheek
at greeting or bedtime you'd give your father, or maybe
rolls an inch or two—depending on the chance of grit,
pebbles, the tilt of ground at this precise point
in the wide world, or the angle of itself it falls on. Not,
however, that *grunt* the condemned man makes
some fifty far-fetched seconds or so
after the injection has done our dirty work, the slump
of his head and just once that grunt as the body
realises its full stop, almost surprised. Nor yet the small
grunt of surprised satisfaction you've heard
when you're as deep inside and around one another
as you two can be, body bearing body away,
and you push, once, and flesh grunts with a right effort
that seems outside, beyond the two of you, something
old and liberated, a sort of joyous punctuation point
in the ravelling sentence that leaves you both as one
breathless wrap of skin and bone, your double weight
hardly anything as you kiss your way down and back
to your own selves, maybe rolling an inch or two
and then lie still, alive, in matter again, the tick of it
starting to fill the silence. But not that either—just a stone
that leaves your opened hand, lets go of you, ascends

---

to its proper pitch this once, and descends, kissing
gravity every inch, to hit the ground you picked it from
with hardly a thought, and staying there, mica stars
glittering in its granite firmament, a stone among stones
in the dust at a verge of meadowgrass and wild carrot.

Date

On this last day of April
flies hatch into flight from moving water,
the surface busy with their glint and speed
and disappearance. Something pink
is flowering in woodshade
where a stray splash of sunlight
finds it, and under the kingfisher's
cratchety rattle the sea alder
comes into pale leaf, crystal pinheads
blaze on short blades of grass
and the long unbroken period
of water over the falls
keeps sounding. Late winter floods
have left fresh revelations: this
clean bank in which a neat
five-fingered print impresses mud,
where the raccoon bent to wash
what moonlit scraps it foraged
from the dark, each splash
a starburst that unsettles peace
with its flash and momentary dazzle,
making, Basho says,
lightning in the water.
Shaking the dew off, two mallards
waddle from high grass
and launch themselves
on creaky wings to water,
then sail away, satisfied
with the light of day, their rings
rippling like connective tissue
to touch and implicate
all the replenished stretch of water
under that mild green flame
the larch starts to figure forth
through its own punctual force
and fine timing.

Spring Fever

As though these fresh leaves
pressed against your brain,
the weather drenching
to the roots of your hair. . . .

Among cloudy forms
a hand fondles a chair-back,
the skin of it
lit as from inside.

Surgery is performed in the early morning:
the station noisy
with headscarves, worry beads, prayers
for a safe, a speedy return.

The procession of yellows goes by,
and in the hot grass
two crimson-gilded flies have stuck
simmering in sunshine, wings ablaze.

The groundhog leaves a sprig
of rummaged green behind,
and a whiskered flicker
digs for live things, blind lives

wriggling under weeds.
Each breath fills empty air
with wings, maple seeds tick
like crickets, the hours darken

into small animals falling
off a cliff. You'd want to push
yourself over like that, to know
the pitch and plummeting descent,

picking things out as you fall:
your cousins' farm, the grey school
behind the mortuary, a wink
of skylights, the white bell tower,

those nameless hands held out
as raining grace. In a sudden
unlikely twist of light
the stacked chairs are gravestones

blazing in the sun, and all day
pacing behind glass you gaze
at a going figure broken by sunlight
and at two women, pale as primroses,

who stand on back steps, arms folded,
speaking into earnest faces.
From this bald height
you can behold your mother

cloaked with age and waving up at you
from a white mound of bones,
and right on time
the plane lurches

across the air, daylight pulses
in the window, the season
fleshes itself
again with sweetness and dread.

Firefly

On my last night in the country, a firefly
gets stuck in the mesh of the windowscreen
and hangs there, revealing to me its tiny legs,
head like a minuscule metal bolt, the beige sac
jutting under its curl of a tail, splayed
on the fine wire and at intervals sparking,
the sac flashing lime green, liquid, electric—
on-off-on, again *on-off-on*, then stop—as if
signalling to me in silence,
the trapped thing singing its own song.

For a while I watched it singing its own song
and then, when it went dark for a long time,
I leaned up close to the wire, to become
a huge looming thing in its eyes, and blew on it
gently, the way you'd blow a faint spark
to fire again—catching a dead leaf, a dry twig,
growing towards flame—and it started to flush
lime green again, *on-off-on* again, deliberate
and slow, a brilliance beyond description
which filled my eyes as if responding to
the bare encouragement of breath I'd offered,
this kiss of life in a lighter dispensation,
as if I'd been part of its alien world
for a minute, almost an element of air
and speaking some common tongue to it,
a body language rarefied beyond the vast
difference between our two bodies, both of us
simply living in this space and making
our own sense of it and, almost, one another.

It's how they talk what we call love to one another
over great distances, making their separate
presences felt in the dark, claiming whatever
the abrupt compulsions of the blood have brought

home to them, then seeking each other out
through the blind static that clogs up the night,
the mob of small voices and hungry mouths
coming between them, that grid of difficulty
they have to deal with if they want in every sense
to find themselves, and decode in their own limbs
the complicated burden of this cold light
they've been, their whole excited lives, carrying.

Of course I don't understand their whole lives carrying
this cold light that might once have been a figure
for the soul, the soul at risk, worn on the sleeve,
its happenstance of chance and circumstance and will,
those habits of negotiation between its own
intermittent radiance and the larger dark; of course
the words I reach to touch it with are clumsy
and impertinent, nothing to the real purpose;
and of course it leads its subtle specific life
beyond these blunderings. But it was the smallest
of all those creatures I've come close to, looked—
however dumbly—into, and was still signalling
that last time I breathed its liquid fire to life,
blew my own breath into its brief body and it fell
from the wire like a firework spending itself
into blackness, one luminous blip of silence into
the surrounding night—the way a firework goes
suddenly silent at its height and drifts back down
in silence, blobs of slow light growing fainter
as they fall into the flattened arms of dark.

But for those moments it inhabited the dark
wired border zone between us, it seemed
as if it could be looking back at me, making
between my breath and its uncanny light
a kind of contact, almost (I want to think)
communication—short, entirely circumscribed,
and set in true perspective by the static-riddled

big pitch dark, but still something like the way
we ourselves might telegraph our selves
in short bright telling phrases to each other:
on-off-on, then stop, the whole live busy night
a huge ear harking to the high notes
of our specific music, and to the silence that
contains it as the dark contains the light.

Swan in Winter

There is this enormous white sleep.
No marks visible on the soft body
sprawled on the saltgrass in a few inches
of rocking water, the long neck
limp as water and flopping back
when you lift and let go, hauling it
out to the solid ground of shells
and seawrack, twilight lights winking
at the wide mouth of the Sound.

Orange beak, black legs and feet
blatant in the mass of white:
the lovely whole creature could be
asleep on the empty shore
in a settled silence dense with questions.
But you've nothing to say to this solid
apparition dropped from a seal grey sky
swollen with snow, the cold
biting through wool and goosedown,
the swan still warm when you
bury your bare hands in whiteness.

That such a great heart could stop
without a sign, those mighty wings
fold over one another for the last time
like that, the live body come to be
just a letting go in the cold, as easy
as entering at first the water, then
take hold of it taking hold and ride
the known currents, companionable
in the friendly element: imagine
those eyes closing, a deeper dark
than their own coming down, this
paschal candle of a bird snuffed out.

There is this solid feel of bone
inside the wing you've opened,
a hinged brightness wide as
a whitewashed wall, the life
seeped out of it, your own hinge-
winged hand the stronger, this huge case
hollow and heavy, immense, bereft,
but ruling in its white absence
the whole foreshore: it is its own
quartz grave, glittering as Newgrange,
and through it all the old swan stories
come floating back, wings singing.

You twist with difficulty
one wingfeather out, pulling
until it comes reluctantly
to hand, lamenting the indignity
but wanting that unfading white
to keep catching light
on your windowsill, contain
this riddling death, this
inexplicable huge conclusion
from purely natural causes.
The pointed quill weighs almost
nothing in your hand, the air in its shaft
electric, each ferny perfect barb
a lit shiver in the breeze.

The chill nips your naked hand
while this deep sleep suffers
no change, although every second
you expect a shuddering roll,
the sleeping beauty to stretch itself
under your touch, the knobbed head
jerk upright, those closed eyes
to open staring into yours
for a moment of pure knowing

as both of you say the one word, *Death*,
to one another, and it will wrench
its white tent of breath and blood
away, its force flooding back, the way

we want resurrections over
and over—of your father fallen back
on his hospital bed, his mouth
gaping after its last breath; your mother
cold in her padded coffin, cheeks
cool as glass, hard as bone;
or your friend sitting cross-legged
on the kitchen floor, a crooked
bloodstring hung from his nose,
hands held open in his lap
as if giving everything away; and you
waiting for their eyes to open
just once more, to say
that all's been known, all understood
at last, all taken in the one embrace
that is the whole body's grace and
affirmation in spite of all, as now

here, again, hoping against hope
the bird will wrench its bones away
and lean up, neck rising like some
great stalk, the head a blossom,
and flatfoot it cumbersome back
to water, wings flowering there
into full sail, and floating on the cold
until it feels fit to change elements
again, and will thrust, run, rise—
its neck riding the sudden loving
surge of air, and rising, *oh*, off and away
into the surprised twilight like a white flame.

But of course it doesn't move
a muscle and you close home
its fanned-out wing and leave it there,

wondering what will happen next—
a high tide take it back, or gulls,
or the rats which inhabit holes in the rocks,
or crows strutting their live
black ravenous appetites all over
this white field.
              Leaving as always
without answers, you see the brisk inlet
lit up by three swans taking off
like gunshot, heraldic wings
hoarding all the light that's left
in the late day, and letting you hear
the musical breath of their beating
as they pass over your head and
swerve inland, as you turn yourself
inland again, past the roofers' hammers
banging echoes up the wooded hill,
and past the red-bellied woodpecker
glimpsed for an instant as it enters,
vanishing, a dead yellow locust.

Border Incident

Near dawn the clear sky is one
big flittering—hosts of pipistrelles
abroad under the paling moon. Not,
to your untuned human ears, a sound
out of their vast assembly—slivers of shadow
silvered by moonlight, livid
hungers on the wing—nor out
of those invisible insects
thronging the air they gorge on.

In the next field, the guns
have been buried for ages
in burlap and paper, protected from rust
under roots of dandelion and delicate thrift,
waiting for this dark form to bend,
dig, draw one out. He straightens,
hardly aims, squeezes the trigger: what
mad scattering, shattered echoes,
the bodies a cloudburst of ripe figs. . . .
As you hurry your children into the cellar,
you hear silence slowly recomposing—
the little one crying, so you carry her,
and herd all in, and bolt the heavy door.

You crouch in the dark and listen:
all over the province
the same thing happens: a noise
entering the world
without warning, the echoes
banging every door with, *Your turn! this time
your turn!* . . . then dying away
to a minute's silence in which you hear
nothing, first, and after—like someone
fumbling a lock—the strange sounds
of your neighbour's breath and steady heartbeat,
the slow tick of church-tower clocks, spires
shivering, the shock of bells.

These Northern Fields at Dusk

(Near Newbliss, County Monaghan)

You'd learn to listen to the big gate
slowly swing in the wind, afloat
on its own all day in a dream of green
and orange light. In the crook
of the hill pasture a scum of flies
has settled on the water
brimming a white cattle trough,
where a congregation of moony eyes
can catch every morning
big-lipped broken glimpses of themselves
gathered together. From the road
you see the whole place
shaped by steel-barred gates
that seem to perch discreetly
on the land—like decorous exchanges
between careful neighbours—
the wildness long ago tamed, trimmed
to use, and garnished with the first
lacy inklings of wild carrot. At this hour
this time of year in this latitude
all the colour that raves by day
gradually leaches out of things, not
towards invisibility but some solid thing—
plain presence—and across the lumpy
quilt of hills you can hear a drumming
ring of metal on metal: someone
hammering a broken pipe or wheel-rim
into better shape. And if you listen
you'll hear whispering: *Nothing
is really lost,* it says, *there is only
this rising up, a shaking out,
a giving back—as these swallows
back from Africa have been given
the swelling heads of grass they shear*

their supper from. This is not the end,
but simply waiting out the waiting itself
until that's the natural state you're in
without fret, a readiness entered: just
walking outdoors—where nothing's changed
for better or worse, but is laid out now
in another light, and being seen by it.

On Fire

How hungrily the wood grown light with weathering
burns, taking its own life until there's nothing left
but blackened fragments on a bed of ash, although it was
all sudden tongues and crackling at the sheer joy
of making its own unmaking like that, this perfumed, rash
expenditure of itself in a reckless cause. I remember
my granny's ramrod back in her widow's weeds,
on her knees in the hearth, bellows in hand, getting
redness to spurt among black coals. Or my mother
laying on their paper bed the sticks of kindling
I'd hatcheted from an orange-box that morning,
arranging the clinker remains of the last fire and
the gleaming nuggets of coal together, then quick
to the kitchen sink, stretching her stained hands
away from her apron. Or my father stacking turf-sods
in the dark mouth of the cottage grate: he'd get
the pale blaze going, then stand back to stare
and say, *There now*, with satisfaction, pour himself
a glass of whiskey, fold open the evening paper,
and sit into the old blue armchair we'd later burn
in the garden. Not discreet but daring, fire has its own
wild fling in the face of gravity, finding its wings and
not looking back, living brilliantly for the moment
it becomes nothing and a handful of ash. The ancients
saw souls in it with the heads of beasts, of birds,
and spent their lives handing it on, as we did
at dawn each Easter morning, quenching every flame
in the church and then—starting from the dark porch—
bringing the new fire into our lives, until the whole place
was ablaze and singing. Unknown soldiers of the world
have poured their own hearts into fire, while houses
of bricks and mortar, steel and glass, have curled up
in the teeth of it like leaves, and blown away. In love,
we are small gods shaking our sandals out as fire,
and at the end we may put our dead in it and gather up
what it makes of them—a few spoonfuls of speckled ash

---

and some bright purged bone. Its truest rhyme
is with *desire*—sprinting to touch, to act, all desperate
reflexive verb. Now the two of us here in the dark
have let the fire die slowly down, and it's your body
I want to see with the curtains open and the half-moon
pressed against the window: your long pale body
smouldering on top of the sheet, glowing beside mine
while we warm ourselves again in the heavy world
of matter, catching fire at the fire we make of our lives.

Ants

A black one drags the faded remains of a moth
backwards over pebbles, under blades of grass.
Frantic with invention, it is a seething gene
of stubborn order, its code containing no surrender,
only this solitary working frenzy that's got you
on your knees with wonder, peering into the sheer
impedimentary soul in things and into
the gimlet will that dredges the dead moth
to where their dwelling is, the sleepy
queen's fat heart like a jellied engine
throbbing at the heart of it, her infants
simmering towards the light. On your table
a tiny red one picks at a speck of something
and hurries away: one of its ancestors
walked all over the eyes of Antinous, tickled
Isaac's throat, or scuttled across the pulse
of Alcibiades, turning up at the Cross
with a taste for blood. In a blink, one enters
your buried mother's left nostril, brings a message
down to your father's spine and shiny clavicle,
or spins as if dizzy between your lover's
salt breasts, running its quick indifferent body
ragged over the hot tract of her, scrupulous
and obsessive into every pore. And here's one
in your hairbrush, nibbling at filaments
of lost hair, dandruff flakes, the very stuff
of your gradual dismantling. Soap, sugar, a pale
fleck of semen or the blood-drop from a mouse
the cat has carried in, it's all one grist to this mill
that makes from our minute leftovers
a tenacious state of curious arrangements—the males
used up in copulation, females in work, life itself
a blind contract between honeydew and carrion,
the whole tribe surviving in that complex gap
where horror and the neighbourly virtues, as we'd say,
adjust to one another, and without question.

Wet Morning, Clareville Road

Under morning greys of rain the roses
are washed, glowing faces, and in near gardens
the limp washing hangs with no hope
although all the slate roofs down Westfield Road
shine like polished chrome. Up early to make
a little door that opens out, a word passage
into the rain-filled air among the flowers
and the morning traffic—as if the words
themselves could offer light, could make
some sense of that muddle in which the heart
flutters. Dark green the overarching
ascension of trees; walled gardens
where scarlet roses are exploding; yellow
the cylinders of chimney pots; luminous
and edgy the fretwork clouds: how things
fall into place from a window, as if the given
were a pattern with precise meanings
and could console us for the loss
of signs, and spires, and words like *consecration,*
or could speak at least a little comfort
after sounding brass, and after
the manic world where men go on
killing as usual, bringing lovely cities down
to rubble, dust. The town of minarets and bells
becomes a cry in the snipered street, hunger
a dog that howls all night, and out
among the hills not too far north of here
the consonantal guns and drums keep beating
and repeating their one word. But here
in our apparent peace there's nothing
but a wet hiss of traffic on glistening road,
the stark green shock of a privet hedge,
that bloodthirsty nude sunburst of roses.

If I went under the rain to smell the roses,
I would inhale your arms, the warm breath

between your breasts, the whole heady
exhalation of you moving by me on the stairs.
Is it because we can't hold onto something
as evanescent as a smell that when it
finds us again it brings the whole body
back into our ready arms: the steady undoing
of straps and buttons, cotton and silk things
drifting from our hot skin, a white shirt
forgetting itself awhile and flying
beyond its own down-to-earth expectations?
Shaken by a slight breeze, lace curtains
let light filter through to the room
I only imagine, where a bowl of roses burns
on a low glass table by the window:
blue mutations agitate air; sea salt
stings the tip of the tongue;
and no ghosts but ourselves to stand
in that early play of light and its solutions
which may contain for the moment
time and all its grazing shades. The room
a flowering branch of details: this
brimming glass, this swimming mirror,
these peaches, this open book, this cracked
black and white Spode bowl, these trials of love.

When that space—with its shades of love
and its impossible colours—fades
to the wet morning outside my window,
I only see the tree in the back garden
bowed down as it is every summer
under a rich crop of bitter little apples.
But my brother makes the garden grow
once more, coaxing its flowers into the sun
like those unhappy patients he'll listen to
all day for their broken stories, crying out with joy
at the first start of the begonia
into pale pink blossom. *I thought it was dead,*
he says without thinking, *and now*

just look at it! He can talk of little else,
learning as he is not to grieve
but go on, and will—when he gets himself
out of bed this morning—fill the house
with his goodwill, looking forward
to whatever happens, ironing his shirts
to the sound of that soprano he loves
singing *Tosca*: when he thinks it's ready,
he'll test the hot iron as our mother would
with a spittled finger, then sing along as he listens
for the startled hiss that steams away
and, like a quick kiss, vanishes.

Shed

You wouldn't know it had been there at all, ever,
the small woodshed by the side of the garage
that a falling storm-struck bough demolished
some seasons back, the space and remains now
overcome by weeds, chokecherry, wild rose brambles.
But, at the verge of where it stood, a peach tree
I'd never seen a sign of before has pushed
its skinny trunk and sparse-leaved branches up
above that clutter into the thoroughfare of light
and given us, this fall, a small basketful
of sweet fruit the raccoons love too and sit at midnight
savouring, spitting the stones down where the shed
used to stand—those bony seeds ringing along
the metal ghost of the roof, springing into the dark.

Notes

page 3   "Statue": A *kouros* in an exhibition called *The Greek Miracle: Classical Sculpture from the Dawn of Democracy*, in the Metropolitan Museum of Art, New York, 1993.

page 19   "Two for the Road": *Shapes:* The (italicised) sentences from the commonplace book are attributed to John Updike. The last sentence in italics is Beckett's. James Day was Professor of Classics at Vassar College.

page 22   "Women Going": Most of these figures refer to pieces of sculpture in *The Greek Miracle.*

page 36   "Visiting Mount Jerome": Mount Jerome is a public cemetery on the south side of Dublin.

page 47   "At the Falls": The phrases in italics are (I believe) from a poem or poems by Marina Tsvetayeva, in the translations of Elaine Feinstein.

page 60   "Angel Looking Away": The pulpit by Giovanni Pisano is in the church of Sant'Andrea in Pistoia.

EAMON GRENNAN is an Irish citizen and the Dexter M. Ferry, Jr.
Professor of English at Vassar College. His previous books include *What
Light There Is & Other Poems* (North Point, 1989) and *As If It Matters*
(Graywolf, 1992). His translations from the Italian poet Giacomo
Leopardi have been published in Ireland by Dedalus Press and are
forthcoming from Princeton University Press. Grennan is the recipient
of a Guggenheim and an NEA fellowship. His work has appeared in
many Irish and American journals, including *Poetry Island Review,* the
New Yorker, the *Nation,* and the *Threepenny Review.*

This book was designed by Will Powers.
It is set in Baskerville and Copperplate Gothic type
by Stanton Publication Services, Inc.
and manufactured by BookCrafters, Chelsea, Michigan
on acid-free paper.
Cover design by Jeanne Lee.